# Paul
# Ride



by Stephanie Wilder
illustrated by Phyllis Pollema-Cahill

Scott Foresman
is an imprint of

PEARSON

Glenview, Illinois • Boston, Massachusetts • Chandler, Arizona
Upper Saddle River, New Jersey

Every effort has been made to secure permission and provide appropriate credit for photographic material. The publisher deeply regrets any omission and pledges to correct errors called to its attention in subsequent editions.

Unless otherwise acknowledged, all photographs are the property of Scott Foresman, a division of Pearson Education.

Photo locators denoted as follows: Top (T), Center (C), Bottom (B), Left (L), Right (R), Background (Bkgd)

Illustrations by Phyllis Pollema-Cahill

ISBN 13: 978-0-328-52150-0
ISBN 10: 0-328-52150-7



11 12 13 V0FL 17 16 15 14

On a chilly April night in 1775, Paul Revere found himself in a small rowboat facing the deep dark of night.

Revere was not afraid. He knew that the message he carried had to reach Lexington before sunrise. The freedom of the colonies rested in Revere's hands. Nothing would stop him from getting his job done.

Earlier that night, Revere's friend Robert Newman had put two lanterns in the bell tower of the Old North Church in Boston. The lanterns would glow in the night sky as a warning to the Sons of Liberty.

The Sons of Liberty was a group that wanted to lead the colonies away from British rule. The two lanterns told them that British soldiers were on their way to Lexington by sea. If Newman had put only one lantern in the bell tower, it would have meant that the British were coming by land. The water route was faster, so Revere would have to work quickly.

Samuel Adams

John Hancock

In case the Sons of Liberty had not seen the **glimmer** of the lanterns, Revere needed to go to Lexington in person to tell Samuel Adams and John Hancock the message. Hancock and Adams were leaders of the Sons of Liberty. Revere wanted to warn them that the British army was coming to arrest them. He also wanted to tell them that the British planned to march on to Concord after stopping in Lexington. The colonial militia, or army, needed to stop them to save the weapons and supplies stored in Concord.

When Revere arrived on the other side of the river, he met with his good friend Deacon Larkin. The deacon was waiting with a strong **steed** to take Revere through the countryside.

Revere climbed onto the horse and set off quickly into the dark night. The journey was long and hard. Revere had trouble seeing where he was going. The darkness **magnified** his fear that he might run into British soldiers, who would surely try to stop him.

Revere was brave, though. He would not let his fears keep him from warning all the people who lived in the villages that the British soldiers were coming.

While Revere was busy making his way to Lexington, the British were busy with their march too. The British troops made their way northwest through the town of Menotomy, which is now called Arlington.

At the same time, another rider named William Dawes was traveling to Lexington with the same message that Revere carried. The two were riding along different roads in case one was stopped by the British.

Just after midnight, both Revere and Dawes arrived safely in Lexington. Revere went straight to the house of Reverend Clark, where Adams and Hancock were staying.

As Revere rode along the path to the house to warn Adams and Hancock, his horse made too much noise, and a colonial guard told him to be quiet. Revere was angry at this and said, "Noise! You'll have noise enough before long." If the British troops were not stopped by the militia in Lexington, there would certainly be more noise when they reached Concord and fought a bigger battle there.

Revere woke Adams and Hancock and told them about the British. Hearing the news, the two men planned to return to Boston within a few hours.

Then Revere met with William Dawes to decide what to do next. They both would ride on to Concord. There they would be able to help in the fight against the British.

Along the way, Revere and Dawes met Dr. Samuel Prescott. Dr. Prescott joined them, and the three men rode on together.

At two o'clock that morning, Revere's biggest worry came true. He and his friends were stopped by British soldiers who were keeping watch over the roads. Dawes and Dr. Prescott were able to get away, but Revere was taken prisoner. The **fearless** Revere would not be held for long, though. He soon began to think of a plan to get away from the British.

The British soldiers asked Revere many questions, but he was very smart. He told them that the British troops would face a battle at Lexington and that they should flee for their lives. The soldiers took Deacon Larkin's horse and gave Revere one of their tired ones. They let Revere go, and he set out again into the dark night alone.

Revere had been on his way to Concord. But now that his strong horse had been taken from him, he decided to head back to Lexington to see if his friends were still there. He reached Reverend Clark's house at three o'clock in the morning, and Adams and Hancock were just preparing to leave. Together the three men made a quick escape.

As they climbed into a stagecoach, Hancock remembered something important. He'd forgotten his trunk at Buckman's Tavern, where he and Adams had stopped earlier that night. The trunk contained important documents that he did not want the British to see. Revere volunteered to retrieve the trunk and told his friends to go on ahead.

It was four-thirty in the morning when he reached the tavern and found the trunk. He was tired and hungry, but he was happy that he had done his part to warn the colonies' leaders. He was relieved that Adams and Hancock were safe and that the trunk was safely in his own hands. Would he make it, though, to fight in the battle that was about to start?

As dawn broke on Lexington Green, the colonial militia lined up to meet the British army. The colonists had only seventy-seven fighting men at Lexington. They would face several hundred British soldiers. The militiamen believed in the colonies' right to rule themselves as much as Revere and the Sons of Liberty did. They stood bravely on the field and awaited their **fate.** It would be the first battle of the American Revolution.

On that **somber** morning in 1775, the colonial militia faced the well-trained British army. Revere listened from a distance as the "shot heard round the world" was fired. The battle for the colonies had begun. The colonists were outnumbered by the British and were forced to retreat. Eight militiamen lost their lives as the British pushed through Lexington Green and on toward Concord.

Later that morning, the British arrived in Concord. But when they got there, they found more than three times as many militiamen as they had faced at Lexington. The fight would not be won as easily this time. The colonists were able to force the British troops back to Boston. They saved their supply of weapons and took an important first step toward freedom.

Paul Revere did not fight in the Battles of Lexington and Concord on that April morning, but he did play a big role. His legend **lingers** in history and is a story that makes Americans feel proud. If he had not braved the dark of night and warned the people of the British attack, the colonists would not have been ready for the fight.

# Glossary

**fate** *n*. things that happen to people that cannot be controlled.

**fearless** *adj*. brave; without fear.

**glimmer** *n*. a faint, unsteady light.

**lingers** *v*. stays.

**magnified** *v*. increased.

**somber** *adj*. serious.

**steed** *n*. a lively horse.